Maike Röder-Thiede

Chinchillas

Everything About Care, Breeding, Health Maintenance, and Nutrition
With a Special Chapter on
Understanding Chinchillas

Advisory Editor: Matthew M. Vriends, PhD

With Color Photographs by Karin Skogstad
and Drawings by Fritz W. Köhler

BARRON'S

New York • London • Toronto • Sydney

All inquiries should be addressed to:
Barron's Educational Series, Inc.
250 Wireless Boulevard
Hauppauge, NY 11788

Library of Congress Catalog Card No. 87-35165

International Standard Book No. 0-8120-4037-6

Library of Congress Cataloging-in-Publication Data

Röder-Thiede, Maike.
    Chinchillas : everything about care, breeding,
health maintenance, and nutrition, with a special
chapter on understanding chinchillas.

        Translation of: Chinchillas.
        Bibliography: p. 54
        Includes index.
        1. Chinchillas.   I. Vriends, Matthew M., 1937-
II. Title.
SF405.C45R6413   1988   636′.93234   87-35165
ISBN 0-8120-4037-6

Printed and Bound in Hong Kong

901 977 98765432

Note of Warning
    This book deals with the keeping and care of
chinchillas as pets. In working with these animals, you
may occasionally sustain minor scratches or bites. Have
such wounds treated by a doctor at once.
    Chinchillas must be watched very carefully during
the necessary and regular exercise period in the house
(see page 23). To avoid life-threatening accidents, be
particularly careful that your pet does not gnaw on any
electrical wires.

Contents

Contents

Preface

Chinchillas, those droll and lively rodents, are native to the Andes of South America. However, since the end of the eighteenth century their pelts have been very much prized, and the resultant intensive hunting has led almost to their extinction in the wild. Not until the 1920s did anyone succeed in breeding them in captivity. Since then chinchillas have mainly been kept and raised for profit on fur farms.

In recent times chinchillas have become more and more popular as pets. Their dainty appearance and soft fur can awaken the desire to have such a cuddly pet. It is important for the chinchilla keeper to have a good understanding of the chinchilla's special care and maintenance needs so that the animal will remain healthy and give its owner many years of pleasure.

This first detailed how-to book makes it easy for the chinchilla keeper to maintain a chinchilla properly in the home. Maike Röder-Thiede—the veterinarian author of this book—discovered her partiality to chinchillas during a visit to a show of fur-bearing animals. She fell in love with a female chinchilla with an almost worthless pelt, whose best prospect was to end up as "buttonhole piping," and she took her home. Since then she has kept and bred chinchillas as house pets. In this book she shares her knowledge and experience and provides expert answers to the many important questions about care and maintenance.

Chinchillas have particular needs that you must understand thoroughly before acquiring one. A chinchilla possesses a pronounced will of its own, which must be respected. It is active at dusk and during the night but needs undisturbed rest during the day. Since it does not become lively until evening, you must play with it then and be sure to allow it sufficient exercise. The chinchilla is not suitable as a cuddly toy for small children. However, a working person can manage a chinchilla well: during the day the animal remains undisturbed, and when you come home in the evening, you find a lively companion.

The author explains how you can provide the living conditions that will maintain the natural life rhythm of the lively, leaping animal. You will learn, as you go through the step-by-step procedure for taming, how to turn the chinchilla into a trusting animal. You receive basic, detailed directions for proper care and feeding, for this is the most important requirement for the animal to feel well and remain healthy. If you have a suspicion that your animal could be sick, the explanations of the possible illnesses and their treatment will be of help.

Anyone who wants to breed pet chinchillas can find here the necessary information about the proper introduction of a pair, mating, gestation, birth, and the development of the young animals.

A chinchilla charms with its artlessness and curiosity. So that you understand your animal and its activity, the author describes the chinchilla's behavior patterns as well as its body language and the sounds it makes.

Filled with clear, up-to-date information, this book is suitable for beginning and more advanced chinchilla keepers.

Author and publisher wish to thank those who have contributed to the success of this book: the photographer Karin Skogstad for the unusual photographs and Fritz W. Köhler for the informative drawings.

When you see a chinchilla for the first time, its droll, dainty appearance is immediately appealing. The roundness of its head and body and its large button eyes awaken motherly, protective feelings—a human instinct that is aroused through the "little child pattern" discovered by the famous biologist Konrad Lorenz. Today chinchillas are more and more frequently offered for sale in pet stores. The chinchilla's appealing looks and its soft fur, which also makes it so desirable commercially, may cause you to wish to possess one. It is instructive to learn how this relatively little-known animal made its way from its native habitat to us.

How Chinchillas Came to Europe and North America

South America is the home of the chinchilla. After the Spanish conquistadors conquered South America in the sixteenth century, the pelt of the chinchilla was introduced to Europe. The softness and thickness of a chinchilla skin was unsurpassed by any other fur. In the eighteenth and nineteenth centuries chinchilla furs were especially sought after. Of course it took over a hundred skins to produce a chinchilla coat. Only a few rich people could afford such a coat, so the hunt for chinchillas in South America was very lucrative.

The First Attempts to Breed Chinchillas

The intensive hunting led to the extinction of the chinchilla in most of its native habitats. Therefore, in the eighteenth and nineteenth centuries, people made the first attempts to breed them in captivity, in Europe as well as in South America—without much luck, however. Successful breeding was not accomplished until the twentieth century. In 1923, in California, an

American mining engineer established a successful brood with about a dozen chinchillas from Chile. With great initial difficulties and bitter setbacks during the next three decades, the so-called ranch breeding of chinchillas was built up in the United States and in Canada. In Germany chinchilla breeding was begun after World War II. Today, millions of chinchillas are bred on fur ranches all over the world.

To carry a chinchilla, hold one hand under its belly and use the other hand to grasp the back firmly.

At first the breeders knew next to nothing about the life needs and the eating habits of chinchillas. Through long experimentation they developed the feeding and maintenance conditions under which these animals remain healthy, live a long time, and quickly reproduce.

Ranch chinchillas are given the minimum necessary living space in their cages. They keep themselves clean and maintain their fur by bathing daily in a sand bath. Calibrated portions of nourishing food encourage good health. Shielded from noise and stress, they are left to themselves like wild animals. As a rule they have little or no contact with human beings and live half-tame in their cages. For fur breeders the skin of the animal is important; other characteristics are of less interest to them.

Chinchillas as Pets

The chinchilla has only become popular as a pet in recent times. Even today, the majority of the animals in human care are living on chinchilla ranches. Selective breeding to rule out hereditary disadvantages or for adaptability to living with human beings does not occur on the breeding ranches. So we have the unusual situation in which a wild animal has been kept for commercial use but has not become a house pet until now.

By standing on its hind legs the chinchilla is able to observe the surroundings attentively.

The Europeans were not the first to discover the chinchilla as a house pet, however. More than 120 years ago, Alfred Edmund Brehm in his famous work *Illustrated Animal Lives* knew enough to report:

"In their native land the large chinchillas are frequently tamed. The gracefulness of their movements, their cleanliness, and the ease with which they adapt to their circumstances soon won them the friendship of human beings. They appear so harmless and trusting that one can let them free in the house and let them run around the rooms. Only through their curiosity do they become troublesome; for they explore everything they find in their path. They may even jump suddenly onto people's heads and shoulders."

Brehm's account shows that chinchillas can be amusing pets. For this to be so, however, it is essential for the chinchilla keeper to learn about the proper care and handling of this furry house companion.

Would a Chinchilla Be Right for You?

Before you bring home a chinchilla, you should consider some basics so that the animal can be comfortable with you and remain healthy.

● Chinchillas are somewhat more expensive to buy and to maintain than other rodents. For instance, they need a large cage.
● Although the chinchilla has been kept and bred as a fur animal for centuries, it has basically remained a wild animal. Something like a cat— even if it has become tame and trusting—it possesses a decided will of its own, which must be respected by its owner.
● A chinchilla is not "teachable," like a dog that you can train. It doesn't learn to protect itself or your home from damage. Therefore you must keep constant watch when it has its free exercise in a room.
● Chinchillas are active at dusk and at night. During the day they must be shielded from the noise and activity of normal family life. When space is limited, you must consider carefully where you can put the cage. A quiet location and a thoroughly soundproofed sleeping box will enable the animal to sleep undisturbed by music,

television, the vacuum cleaner, and other daytime noises. Chinchillas can become overstrained by stress, such as that brought about by loud sounds or excitement, and can even die of a sudden heart attack. You would certainly want to ensure that it can spend a proper long life of 10 to 15 years with you (the outside life expectancy is about 18 to 22 years).

● Be aware that the noise the chinchillas make in the night by rustling, digging, nibbling, and gnawing can disturb you. You must either sleep so well that these noises don't bother you, even if the cage is in the room in which you sleep, or you must have some way to avoid it—even in a one-room apartment—perhaps by putting the cage in the hallway at night. Bathrooms are less suitable places for the cage because the noise of the flushing toilet will frighten the animal (see The Right Location, page 17).

● Even working people, singles or couples, can keep a chinchilla. The animal is undisturbed during the day, and when you come home in the evening, it will just be coming awake.

One or Two?

Keeping one animal is easy with chinchillas. With proper care and through your capacity for sympathetic understanding, the chinchilla will soon become trusting and inquisitive. If you give it its exercise every evening and play with it, even a single chinchilla will be happy.

Keeping two chinchillas is somewhat more difficult. In the first place, the cage for two animals must be substantially larger. In a cage that is too small, the chinchillas get on each other's nerves at times, and this can lead to behavioral disturbances, such as fur biting (see page 37). Two female animals that are brought up together often do well together, as will a mother and daughter. Two male chinchillas, like unacquainted females, will not tolerate each other.

For keeping a pair the largest cage possible is an important requirement. As a rule a male and female tolerate each other quite well. But what about breeding? Two, possibly three, litters can be expected each year, each litter with one to three or even four babies. The circle of suitable friends and acquaintances who will take them is soon saturated. Then there remains only a trustworthy pet dealer who can sell your baby chinchillas. All things considered, it is probably best to have the male neutered. For this you must find an experienced veterinarian or go to an animal hospital.

Male or Female?

The sex of the chinchilla is not important if you are going to keep only one. Males are more often available in pet stores or from breeders because the females are kept for breeding (see Sex Determination, page 15).

Children and Chinchillas

As much as chinchillas seem like lap animals because of their cuddly soft fur, they are by no means suitable as cuddly pets for smaller children. Guinea pigs make better pets for young children. Children must be older to enjoy observing and playing with the cute little chinchillas. At about the age of 13 they are usually old enough to take responsible care of them. For instance, they must know that one shouldn't feed the animal a lot of treats that are not good for it.

Top and bottom, a pair in the color mutations brown and brown velvet; bottom left, the brown male, 11 years old; bottom right, the brown velvet female, 10 years old.

Before You Buy

They must also understand that a chinchilla needs its rest until the early hours of the evening. In any case the adult members of the family must be ready to offer guidance and to help with the chinchilla care, particularly if children lose interest in the animal and neglect it.

Chinchillas and Other Pets

Basically I advise against keeping a chinchilla with other pets. It's difficult to keep chinchillas in a room or even in a cage with other pets. Problems that can develop are: stress, wounds, and digestive disturbances. In certain instances the animals can tolerate each other (animals that cannot tolerate each other must be separated at once!).

Above all you must make certain that none of your other animals disturb the daytime rest of the chinchillas.

Birds: that make noise all day cannot be kept in the same room with your chinchilla. Also, it would drive a chinchilla into a panic if the bird were to sit on its cage.

A dog: that constantly barks and snuffles around the cage gets on the chinchilla's nerves. You must know yourself if you can control your dog's behavior toward a chinchilla and can train the dog. For instance, it will certainly not please the chinchilla if the dog puts its paw on the chinchilla in play or if it barks at all. A chinchilla may get used to a quiet, well-behaved dog, however, even to the point of exercising while it is in the same room.

A cat: may cause similar problems. A chinchilla is really not robust enough for a game. Be careful if the cat "playfully" swipes at the chinchilla with a paw and at the same time lets its claws out a little. The chinchilla's large eyes are in danger.

The 5-year-old white chinchilla Pablo, standing on his hind legs.

Rodents: kept together in one cage with a chinchilla produce two basic problems: the different day and night activities of the individual animals and the different feeding habits. A very active or noisy animal will disturb the chinchilla. As for feeding, experience has unfortunately demonstrated that all other feed tastes better to the snacking chinchilla than the roughage-rich diet intended for it.

I consider a common cage with mice, rats, or gerbils extremely unhealthy for a chinchilla. With their activity day and night and their constant scurrying around they drive a chinchilla crazy in short order. The golden hamster is a loner and is not to be considered for keeping with a chinchilla for that reason.

A guinea pig: on the other hand, will often be tolerated without difficulty by a chinchilla. The chinchilla immediately accepts this alien species as a companion in a common cage. This occurs because in their natural habitat chinchillas live peacefully with other rodents—like the chinchilla rat—in common caves and rock crevices (see The Home, page 48). A guinea pig will offer the chinchilla no competition in the upper regions of the cage, which must be very high—at least 39 inches (1 m), for climbing branches and sitting boards—or in the sleeping house.

The big problem is the feed: The chinchilla loves to eat the guinea pig's food and gets indigestion from it.

Dwarf rabbits: produce the same feeding problems as guinea pigs. But the biggest problem arises from the behavior patterns of the dwarf rabbit. The males regard all other animals as sex objects. Constant vigorous attempts to mate will terrify a chinchilla. Even a neutered pygmy rabbit buck is often uncommonly aggressive—at least when it comes to territorial boundaries in the cage area. Again and again he will attack his fellow occupant to defend his territory. The dwarf rabbit doe is particularly aggressive and, most important of all, unpredictable during the nest-building phase of her false pregnancy. The pygmy rabbit's lightning-fast attack and scratching forefeet can inflict severe eye injury on a chinchilla. Aside from this, the sudden attacks produce a state of constant uneasiness and insecurity in the chinchilla.

What to Do with a Chinchilla During Vacation

Before you buy a chinchilla, consider carefully who will take care of the animal during your vacation (or your absence for other reasons, such as illness or business trips).

I advise against taking a chinchilla away on vacation with you. Long automobile trips and the resulting multiple changes of surrounding are too upsetting for the animal. For a few days of absence you can leave the animal in its cage. Every day, toward evening, it must be cared for by a responsible person. If this caretaker is comfortable

with the behavior of your chinchilla and the animal behaves trustingly with this strange person, it can also be allowed to exercise in the room for a while in the evening.

During an absence of several weeks, the evening run and a little play with the animal are very important. If a chinchilla has too little freedom of movement, it quickly becomes constipated (see page 34) or may develop a behavioral disturbance (see Fur Biting, page 37). If the chinchilla must be transferred to other living quarters during your absence, it should find its own familiar cage there. The necessary shielding of the chinchilla must be arranged. It should only be allowed to run around loose when it acts serene and normal again in its new surroundings.

In any case, write down the necessary information about care and feeding for the caretaker so that your chinchilla will lack for nothing while you are away.

Buying Advice

Where You Can Get Chinchillas

Pet stores: Go to a dealer who gives customers individual attention. If the dealer doesn't have chinchillas or doesn't handle them, he or she can surely get you an animal from a nearby fur farm or hobby breeder. If your chinchilla comes to you in this simple way, it will be spared a great deal: long journeys, multiple changes of surroundings, and many changes of diet. Long trips from the breeder to the owner place great stress on the chinchilla to begin with. Furthermore, these intermediate stops can endanger the animal's health through the possible concentration of germs in mixed groups of animals and in cages that are continuously reused for animals from different sources. It is best to give the chinchilla the same diet as the breeder or handler gave it. If it has had the right feed (see page 30), take enough of it with you to last for at least the first week.

A long-tailed chinchilla (*Chinchilla lanigera*). This species with its slender body and large ears was the principal ancestor of our pets.

Fur breeders: Perhaps you can find a chinchilla ranch in your neighborhood. They will certainly sell you a superfluous male from their brood; they are not so eager to part with healthy females. The breeder will also gladly give you advice for keeping your chinchilla. On the smaller chinchilla ranches a family member usually looks after raising the young. Lovingly brought up young animals are used to the human hand and will therefore tame more quickly.

Hobby breeders: Because chinchillas are becoming ever more popular as pets, it may be that a hobbyist in your neighborhood has found that he or she has a mating pair and would be glad to be able to give up some of the babies into loving hands. From a hobbyist's experience with chinchillas you can learn many useful tips.

You can contact chinchilla farmers and hobby breeders through your local pet store.

What You Should Look for When Buying

No matter where you buy your chinchilla, it's important that before buying you pay attention to the cleanliness of the cages and the condition of the animal's health.

Chinchillas should be kept in rooms that are bright, dry, and not too warm. An animal by itself is easy to judge if you observe certain signs. If chinchillas are offered in large groups or with guinea pigs and pygmy rabbits, it's much more difficult to observe and to examine a single animal. Still, it's even more important in this case to allow yourself time and to observe enough before you decide on an animal. Never rush into buying an animal! Sit by the cage and watch the chinchilla that pleases you.

During the day chinchillas doze quietly in a corner or in their sleeping house. It's hard at these times to tell whether an animal is healthy. It's best to go to the pet store shortly before closing time. Perhaps the chinchillas will already have become lively.

Signs of possible illness: for which you should watch if you are observing the chinchilla are as follows.

Buying Advice

If a chinchilla sits withdrawn in a corner and doesn't eat, it is probably sick, without your being able to determine anything more precisely. Wait until dusk, however, to judge to see if the chinchilla becomes more active.

● Crust and scaliness at the nose, eyes, and ears are symptoms of a skin fungus (see page 35). Most fungus diseases can be communicated to human beings.

● If you notice that the feces of a singly kept animal are very small (see drawing, page 33), it has constipation (see page 34).

● Runny nose and streaming eyes are signs of a cold (see page 35).

● Flowing saliva and slow or excessive chewing movements suggest unhealthy teeth anomalies (see page 36). As a rule they lead to the starvation of the animal.

Other important signs: By all means ask the seller or the breeder to take the chinchilla you are interested in out of the cage. When it is held in the hand, you can examine it from all sides and also touch it. Watch for the following:

● The placement and the length of the incisor teeth must be normal (see drawing, page 25).

● Whitish, transparent incisor teeth are a sign of malnutrition.

● A dirty anal region indicates diarrhea (see page 33).

● Emaciation is a sign of a bad diet or of serious illness. Chinchillas are slender under their thick fur. If with gentle palpation you can feel notably protuberant vertebrae, cheekbones, and ribs, the animal is too thin.

● Holes in the fur are a sign of a behavioral disturbance in the animal, of "fur-biting" (see page 37).

Note: Should even one animal in any group of animals show signs of an illness, I would advise you not to buy a chinchilla from this group. The animals may have already infected one another without symptoms being visible yet.

The Age of the Chinchilla When You Buy It

Young chinchillas are separated from the mother at the age of 7 to 8 weeks. They stay with the

To examine the incisors, hold the chinchilla firmly with one hand; with the other hand grasp the head and pull the upper lip up and the lower lip down.

The chinchilla is lifted up by the base of the tail for sex determination or for removal of hair rings from a male.

14

Buying Advice

breeder for 2 to 4 weeks more until they are strong and hardy. Chinchillas in the pet store are mostly 3 to 6 months old. Chinchillas vary in size, so you can't tell their age by looking. In grown animals, males are usually somewhat smaller than females. So ask your dealer or the breeder about the age of the chinchillas that are being offered. On the whole I would advise you to get a young animal because these tame more quickly. It doesn't make much difference, however, whether the animal is barely 3 months or already 6 months old.

Sex Determination

It's best if you have the difference demonstrated and explained by the pet dealer or the breeder. At first look, the female and the male genital parts look very much alike. Thus I originally thought that my Amadea, which was the first chinchilla that was "born to me," was an Amadeus. I confused the female urinary tube opening, which protrudes like a little spigot, with the male penis. In the drawing the distinctions are clear: in the female the anus, the transversely positioned vagina, and the outlet of the urinary tube are situated closely together, whereas in the male there is a small space between the anus and the penis.

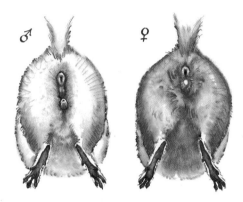

In the male (left) there is a small space [about 0.4 inches (1 cm)] between the anus and the penis. In the female (right) the anus and the spigot ending of the urinary tract lie very closely together. Between them is the transverse vagina, which is not visible and opens only during estrus.

Housing and Equipment

The Right Cage

You should arrange for the housing of your chinchilla well before you set out to buy the animal. Don't practice false economy when it comes to the equipment, and don't skimp on the cage, especially. The chinchilla is a very lively animal and loves to jump. Proper care and maintenance require the largest living space possible. A cage can very easily be too small but never too large. This is important because the chinchilla must spend the time that it is most active—that is, nighttime—in the cage. A fur breeder tries to achieve numerous offspring and optimal fur quality at the least possible expense. Anyone who keeps a chinchilla as a house pet should place greater value on appropriate living accommodations.

Important Cage Features

No matter what cage you decide on, there are certain features that every chinchilla cage should have if the animal is to feel comfortable in it. You should also consider when you choose a cage how you are going to clean it.

Grating: The chinchilla can't gnaw galvanized grating or galvanized wire mesh. Metal can easily be cleaned of dust and hairs. A chinchilla cage should not have lacquered or plastic-coated grating, which could cause digestive upset if the chinchilla gnaws on it.

Floor surface: A floor surface of metal is most convenient. The cage can have a plastic floor if the chinchilla can't gnaw the surface. In any case, it's better if the floor has a built-in drawer in it (perhaps of galvanized tin) because it makes the work of cleaning substantially easier.

Cage door: A large cage door is practical; it allows you to remove the dust bath, the food dish, and the sleeping house from the cage without difficulty.

Caution: A chinchilla that is jumping around can injure itself badly on sharp corners, soldered joints, nails, screws, and brackets. Nails and brackets that have been exposed by gnawing should be removed.

The chinchilla needs a daily bath in special dust to clean its coat.

Dimensions

I have compared different cages and their sizes. Those used by chinchilla ranchers as breeding cages have dimensions of 19.5×19.5×19.5 inches (50×50×50 cm) (height × width × depth). A special chinchilla cage can be found at the pet dealer's. It has dimensions of 17.5×26.5×14 inches (45×68×36 cm). The height of the special cage is less than that of the breeding cages. Therefore this chinchilla cage is suitable only for transporting the animal. You can use it to take the chinchilla to the veterinarian if it is sick, or to friends who are going to look after it while you are away. The "chinchilla house" offered by pet dealers has the advantage of being somewhat roomier, with its dimensions of 20×27×17.5 inches (51×70×45 cm). It has a bottom tray of metal.

Housing and Equipment

The chinchilla cage is available in pet stores. A chinchilla can live in this cage if daily it is allowed to run free in the room.

Recommended Cages

Aviaries for small birds are more suitable as cages for chinchillas. For a single animal a height of 39 inches (1 m), a width of 31 to 39 inches (80 to 100 cm), and a depth of 19.5 inches (50 cm) are sufficient (see drawing, page 17). The plastic floor drawer that is supplied with the aviary is not suitable. Chinchillas gnaw, and chips and the eating of large quantities of plastic can be lethal for the animal. Plastic parts that the animal can gnaw absolutely do not belong in a chinchilla cage! Have a drawer made to order from galvanized or aluminum-coated tin by a plumber. Aviaries for small birds have wire mesh with a gauge of 0.6 inches (14 mm). Even newborn chinchillas can't get through mesh this size.

If you want to dig somewhat more deeply into your pocket you can buy a larger aviary for small birds. They have dimensions of 66×31×19.5

inches (170×80×50 cm). These cages have a plastic-coated back wall. In place of the plastic drawer that is supplied you must also have a floor drawer of galvanized or aluminum-coated tin made. You can keep a small colony of chinchillas in this roomy home, but a single animal will certainly be thrilled to have so much freedom to move.

Protective Covering

Outside the back wall and on both side walls of the cage you should attach plastic-coated panels, which will shelter the chinchilla from drafts. The animal will also not be disturbed if someone moves behind or alongside the cage. If you have a cat or a bird that can move freely in the room, you must be sure to attach a panel to the top of the cage, too. The cat and the bird will be sure to sit on the cage—but this can frighten a chinchilla to death. Its instinct makes it flee from any movement over its head. In nature this flight reaction often saves the animals from hawks and other predators (see Natural Enemies, page 49).

The Right Location

The location of the chinchilla cage must meet specific requirements if the chinchilla is to be comfortable and not to suffer from any disturbing or health-damaging influences. Note the following points:

● The room in which the cage stands must be dry but not too warm. Be sure not to overheat the room in winter. Chinchillas feel best at temperatures between 59 and 64°F (15 and 18°C).
● The cage must not stand in a draft!
● The location must be well lit, but the sun should not shine directly onto the cage or the temperature in the cage will rise too high. The chinchilla might suffer a heat stroke.

Housing and Equipment

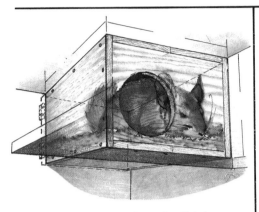

The chinchilla can get its daily rest in a little house with an entry hole like this one.

• If the room in which the cage stands must be used during the day, find a quiet, protected corner in which to place it.
• Place the cage against the wall. If you are constantly moving around the cage because it is in the middle of the room, the chinchilla will become nervous and anxious.
• Don't put the cage on the floor! It's best if it sits about chest high, possibly even on or in a bookcase. The cage must be high enough so that you can't bend over it, which would terrify the animal. A shy chinchilla will sit up in the corner of a cage. Allow it this chance to retreat. Having your face always appear at the same level will reassure it.

Arrangement of the Cage

Sleeping house or box: A house for the chinchilla to sleep in is essential. It's best if it's a small house, closed on all sides, and has only a small entry hole. The chinchilla can get its required rest inside. Closed guinea pig houses with an entry hole or breeding boxes for cockatiels also make suitable sleeping houses. The sleeping house should be placed on the highest sitting board and firmly anchored, or it will fall down with the chinchilla's romping. You can screw it to the cage mesh or fasten it between the perching board and the roof.

A drainage tile [diameter 6 inches (15 cm); length at least 8 inches (15 cm)] can also serve as a sleeping house, but these are difficult to fasten to perching boards.

If your chinchilla prefers to sleep on the floor—you'll notice that in the mornings it doesn't enter its sleeping house but remains sitting on the floor in the straw—you can lay such a drainage tile in the straw. In this case, if there is a sleeping house on a perch, you should take it down and place it on the cage floor.

The sleeping house should be cushioned with straw.

Water dispenser: Buy a rabbit or hamster water dispenser. They have a tank and a little water pipe of glass. This material is best for the chinchilla and is easy to clean. The dispenser is

The spout of the water dispenser should be fastened outside the cage mesh just high enough that the chinchilla can drink out of it comfortably.

fastened outside the cage mesh, and the drinking pipe is stuck through the mesh into the cage. If you leave a distance of 8 inches (20 cm) between the end of the pipe and the cage floor, the chinchilla can drink comfortably. Don't put the water dispenser over the hayrack! Water dropping into the hay rots it.

Hayrack: You should hang a hayrack of galvanized wire inside the cage along the mesh. A rabbit rack is big enough to hold the daily hay ration for the chinchilla. You can also fill a hardwood box with hay and stand it on the cage floor.

Food bowl: Get a heavy food bowl of clay or pottery from the pet store. The chinchilla will tip over a food bowl that is small and light and make a mess as it hops around.

Bathtub: A container for the daily bath in special dust is an essential part of the basic equipment. It should be somewhat bigger than the chinchilla, so that the animal can turn comfortably and can roll around. Breeders have bathtubs of sheet zinc, but a high-walled tub of clay or pottery will do as well. The tub must be stable and gnaw-proof.

Litter: You can use small-animal litter of wood or corn cob shavings that you get from the pet shop for the floor and the sleeping house. The cage floor should be covered with about 2 inches (5 cm) of litter. (Avoid wood shavings that have been chemically treated and cedar shavings, which contain resin that may be harmful to chinchillas.)

Sitting places: Depending on the size of the cage, you should attach one or two boards, level horizontally, to the walls of the cage. Either use shorter boards on the side walls or longer, narrow boards on the back side of the cage (see drawing, page 18). The boards can be hung on the fencing with hooks or fastened firmly to the wooden walls with angle irons. You can divide the cage into different "floors" with these boards. Your chinchilla should be able to make jumps of 12 to 20 inches (30 to 50 cm) from one board to the other or to the floor. Use untreated pine or beech for the sitting boards.

Climbing branches: You can fasten climbing branches between the perching boards and the cage walls (see drawing, page 20). The branches should be of beech, willow, hazelnut bushes, pine, or fruitwood (you must not use branches from elder bushes). Use only branches from untreated and unsprayed trees. These branches should also not have grown near a well-traveled road. The more climbing branches you provide for the chinchilla, the more gnawing material it has at its disposal. It will also be less likely to gnaw the sleeping house and perches to pieces too soon.

Gnawing stone: A gnawing stone is beneficial to a chinchilla if it does not have enough other gnawing material in its cage. The pet shop carries a gnawing stone made especially for chinchillas.

The Homemade Cage

If you have some manual skill you can build a cage for a chinchilla yourself. Specifically you will need:

- plastic-coated masonite boards for the walls, roof, floor, and drawer
- strips of lumber for the framing for the front side and for the cage door
- galvanized mesh [gauge about 0.5 inches (14 mm)]
- tin strips to cover open joints
- pine or beech boards for the sleeping house and perches
- hinges and bolt for the door, wood screws or dowels, staples for fastening the mesh, angle irons or hooks for fastening the perches

The walls of the cage, roof, and floor will be put together with wood screws or wood dowels.

Housing and Equipment

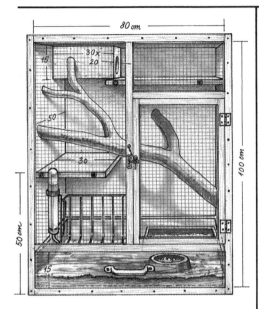

A home-made cage that provides enough room and variety for the chinchilla.

The same is true of the floor drawer and the frame for the front side. All joints are sealed with silicon glue so that no urine can get into the wood. The upper edges of the drawer are protected with tin strips. The strips are bent around the corners and nailed fast. Instead of building a drawer with boards, you can also have one made of galvanized tin by a plumber. This will save you some work and will simplify cleaning later.

Attach the wire mesh to the inside of the framework with a staple gun and a tack.

In the pet store ready-made cage fronts are available in different sizes. These ready-made elements will spare you the work of having to build the front of the cage. Get advice from the dealer.

The door is attached to the front edge with hinges (outside!) and equpped with a secure bolt.

You can put together a sleeping house with wooden dowels. Nails or screws are less suitable here; the chinchilla can uncover them with gnawing and can injure itself on them.

Care and Maintenance

Taking the Chinchilla Home

If you have a long trip, it's preferable to put the chinchilla in a small, gnaw-proof cage. Perhaps you can borrow a bird or guinea pig cage if you don't have one yourself. The chinchilla will gnaw through even a rugged cardboard carton in minutes, so you can use such a container only if someone else in the car can keep an eye on the escape-happy chinchilla. I once learned at first hand how stress producing a curious, enterprising chinchilla in the passenger's seat can be for one driving alone on a very short car trip: one hand on the steering wheel, one eye on the traffic, and the other hand and the other eye busy with the chinchilla, which scouted its unfamiliar surroundings with astonishing calm.

So that the animal won't be irritated by unfamiliar noises from outside or by changing light conditions, the cage should be covered with a cloth or a cover. Be careful; the little animal may eat the cloth (which can cause a digestive upset).

Adaptation

The cage should already be set up when the new occupant arrives (see Housing and Equipment, page 16). A filled food dish and a water dispenser should also be there before you put your chinchilla in the cage, so that it can be left in quiet when it is first placed in its new home.

Proceed with *placement in the cage* as carefully as possible: Hold the transport container (or the transport cage) with the opening next to the open cage door so that the curious animal can enter its new home on its own initiative. Be calm and patient. If this method doesn't succeed in moving the chinchilla, take the animal gently in both hands. Don't hurry. So that it doesn't escape you, gently hold the base of the tail firmly with the thumb and forefinger of one hand, using the other hand to grasp it under the belly (see Proper Lifting and Carrying, page 22). Put it into the cage. Don't worry; if the animal doesn't panic and if the surroundings are quiet, it usually won't bite. Then close the cage door. You can now observe from a distance how the chinchilla explores its new surroundings.

The First Days

For the next few days and weeks you should be very cautious in dealing with the animal. How long the chinchilla needs to feel at home depends on how tame it was before and its individual timidity. Confine all necessary care measures, like feeding and cleaning work, to the absolute minimum. You should perform any tasks in the evening, during the animal's normal waking period. As a rule, the chinchilla will react somewhat cautiously or anxiously if you are in the vicinity of the cage or if you (carefully and quietly!) attempt to do anything inside it. Move slowly, without crowding the chinchilla, and speak quietly to it. Give the chinchilla time! Every unnecessary fright only lengthens the taming period.

Perhaps in the beginning you won't be able to tell that the chinchilla is active at dusk and at night. Any curious young animal will react at any time of day to everything that goes on outside or inside its cage. Don't respond to its curiosity in the daytime and don't speak with it. Simply act as if the chinchilla didn't exist at all. You will see how quickly the animal learns that nothing important happens in the daytime. Soon it will recover its natural sleeping time. This is important, because any activity during the day is not in accord with its innate life rhythms and therefore means stress and injury to the animal.

Care and Maintenance

Taming the Chinchilla

For your chinchilla to become tame and trusting, you must gradually get it used to your hands and to your body. Therefore it is important that you carry out the following taming practices slowly, step by step. Only when one stage of tameness is achieved should you go on to the next.

Fence tameness: As soon as the curious chinchilla comes up to the cage mesh in the evening, quietly begin to offer it treats (see page 30) and small pieces of calcium tablet (see page 31) through the wire. Speak with it while you are doing this. Soon the chinchilla will be trusting enough to take these treats from your fingers.

Food tameness: Once your chinchilla shows no more anxiety at the fence, open the cage door. Make sure that the animal can't jump out. Now hold out the treat. If the chinchilla eats from your fingers without hesitation, then as a next step lay the treat on the flat of your hand. Hold your hand utterly still until the animal dares to place its front feet on your hand and take the food. Then, when that is accomplished, lay the food on your forearm, which you hold quietly in the cage. The chinchilla will also climb onto your forearm to get the food. It takes much patience until the animal has overcome its timidity. Give yourself and the chinchilla time until everything goes along as a matter of course.

Complete tameness: For the chinchilla to be at ease with your body, too, lean your trunk into the open cage door and let the chinchilla explore your arms and clothes. Give it food when it sits on your arm.

The next step is to hold one hand over the chinchilla's body, so that it gets used to the grip. When it shows no more anxiety about your hand, reward it with an especially nice treat while you take hold of it. If the animal perches on your arm or your chest, once in a while try taking one step back from the cage and then letting it hop into the cage again. Be careful that

the chinchilla doesn't spring away from you into the room.

Practice: Practice all these steps from fence tameness through complete tameness slowly and often. These taming practices must "stick" before you can allow the animal to exercise. The chinchilla must be comfortable with your hands and your body. This way no upsetting chase can develop if later you want to put the animal back in its cage after exercise. In hectic capture situations the chinchilla loses its trust of human beings.

To lift and carry, grasp the chinchilla carefully at the base of the tail with one hand underneath and carry it on your hand or your forearm.

Proper Lifting and Carrying

When you have the feeling that your chinchilla is really trusting and shows no fear at all when grasped by your hands, you should begin to carry it around. Therefore you must practice holding the animal fast if it is sitting on your hand. To do so, place your thumb at the base of its tail (see drawing) to keep it from springing away unex-

Care and Maintenance

Keeping your thumb at the base of the tail keeps the chinchilla from springing out of your hand.

pectedly. Then the other hand is enough to carry it. These carrying practices should be done only for seconds at first and can be extended later, but only when the animal has gotten used to them.

If you want to determine the sex of a chinchilla (see page 15) or to remove hair rings from the penis of a male (see page 26), you must lift the chinchilla at the base of the tail. Please, never catch a chinchilla by the tail base! First take it in both hands, and then grasp the base of the tail and let the chinchilla hang from this support (see drawing, page 14). You should only use this method of holding the chinchilla when it is absolutely necessary because the animal doesn't like it.

Caution: Never grasp or hold the chinchilla by the end of its tail! Not only the fur but the entire very delicate tail end can break off this way!

Daily Exercise

The chinchilla must be completely tame before it can have its daily free—and at first very care-fully supervised—exercise. It's best if you begin with it on a table, which you place before the cage and at a height the chinchilla can master. You can keep it from jumping off the table by diverting it with food. To do so, sit at the edge of the table so that the animal, instead of jumping down, climbs on you instead. Practice for several days and then place next to the table a chair onto which the chinchilla can hop. Continue to let the animal climb on your body in the meantime. These are important preparations for running free in the room. The chinchilla should gladly return to you for treats so that it can be replaced in its cage without difficulty at any time.

Dangers for the Chinchilla

Before you finally and definitely let the chinchilla explore the room, examine the room carefully for visible and concealed hazards (see Table of Hazards, page 24). For example, wires and houseplants should be removed from the immediate range of the animal. Hiding places that can be reached only with difficulty by humans, such as the space behind the refrigerator, cupboards, or ovens, should be blocked off ahead of time. The chinchilla's free run in living areas is really only possible under constant supervision, if neither the chinchilla nor your furniture is to come to harm. Please don't try to train the animal or to break it in at all. With a chinchilla you have taken a wild animal for a house companion, not a dog. Hissing, whistling, or clapping will certainly stop the animal for a moment from proceeding with an undesirable or dangerous activity, because it's frightened. However, it basically never learns not to do these things. Always remember: Strong fear increases stress for the chinchilla and makes it nervous and frantic. If you want to keep the animal from gnawing on your furniture, for example, hold out a branch for it to gnaw on; perhaps it will find it just as interesting and tasty.

Care and Maintenance

Hazard	Consequences	Avoiding the Hazard
Washing and cleaning materials, chemicals, medicines	Poisoning, often fatal; acid burns	Put away cleaning and washing materials, chemicals, and medicines; let washed floors dry
Filled bathtubs, pails, and large vases	If the chinchilla falls in and you don't notice, it will drown	Keep the bathroom door closed during the chinchilla's exercise period; cover filled containers
Washing machines	Being closed inside and drowning	Keep the washing machine closed; check the drum before using
Electrical wires	Death from shock on gnawing; also dangerous for the pet owner	Block access to concealed wires; be sure exposed wires are not connected.
Houseplants, cut flowers	Poisoning through chewing or eating; injuries from cactus	Place plants out of reach, or take them out of the room during exercise period
Open and "cracked" windows	Escape, falls; caught in falling windows	Close all windows during exercise
Kitchens	Burns on stoves and from jumping or falling into kettles, pots, pans, or dishwater; digestive upsets from licking remains of food; stuck fur from fats	Close the kitchen door during exercise, or allow the chinchilla into the kitchen only when it is clean
Fruit bowls, plates of sweets, onions, and garlic	Digestic disturbances if the chinchilla nibbles on them	Place bowls and containers in a cupboard, or take them out of the room during exercise
Dogs, cats (visiting animals)	Bites, shock, or even death of the chinchilla	Preferably keep other animals out of the way during the chinchilla's exercise period
Doors, cupboard doors	Injury from pinching; getting shut in; escape	Watch the chinchilla if doors or cupboard doors are used
Human feet	Crushing and broken bones from being stepped on	Exercise extreme caution; especially with small children!
Filled ashtrays	Tobacco poisoning	Don't leave any full ashtrays around
Heaters, sunlamps	Burns through hopping onto them	Turn off equipment, and let it cool before the exercise period
Furniture	Crushing and broken bones from being sat on	Look before sitting on any seat
Stained and lacquered wood	Irritability or poisoning after gnawing	Prevent any gnawing at all: distract the chinchilla!
Textiles, plastics, plastic bags	Irritability, constipation, or poisoning after gnawing; suffocation.	Do not leave any dangerous materials where the animal can get at them

Care and Maintenance

Playing with the Chinchilla

Playing with your new household companion consists to a large degree in observation of its activities. It will very soon explore all the "highs and lows" of your home in its hopping way of locomotion, testing many things for edibility (careful!) and delighting you with its curiosity and artlessness. When it has romped around the room a little, it will certainly happily bounce its way back to you. Some chinchillas then try to cuddle and snuggle up to a human and prove to be real petting animals. This need is more strongly pronounced among some individuals than others, however.

Care of the Chinchilla

The caretaking procedures that follow are very important for the well-being and the health maintenance of the chinchilla.

Fur Care

Chinchillas are very clean animals and care for their fur themselves. To do so, they use a daily dust bath. For about 30 minutes every evening, place in your chinchilla's cage an appropriate container (see page 19) as a bathtub filled with special dust. The chinchilla will turn and roll in it. The special dust for chinchillas is finer than any bird sand and cannot really be replaced by anything else. Ask in your pet store about this special item. Without these daily dust baths, the chinchilla's fur loses its fragrance and becomes greasy and sticky or even matted. If your chinchilla likes to have you stroke it, the fur will become greasy that much faster. The daily bath in the proper special dust is especially important in this case.

Tooth Care

The teeth of rodents, chinchillas among them, grow continually. The chinchilla must continually grind down its incisors so that they maintain the right length and shape. Therefore you must put branches (always new ones) in the cage for the chinchilla to gnaw on. In addition you can put a gnawing stone from the pet store into the cage.

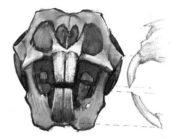

To keep its teeth the right length and shape, the chinchilla regularly needs suitable gnawing material.

From time to time examine the growth and the placement of the incisors (see drawing). You can also tell by the way the chinchilla eats if its incisors are not in order: Very slow eating or stopping while eating are signs that something is not right. To examine the incisors, take the chinchilla in your left hand so that the thumb is placed below the lower jaw. With the right hand enclose the head and lift the upper lips; then with the left hand draw down the lower lip a little (see drawing, page 14).

Examination of Feces

Constant supervision of its digestion is important for the health of the chinchilla. Examine the feces daily, and pay attention to the first sign of a digestive disturbance. The appearance of the feces of healthy and sick animals is depicted in a drawing (see page 33). Feces that are in small

Care and Maintenance

balls are signs of constipation (see page 34). If the feces are so soft that they are pressed flat by the chinchilla and leave green smears on the litter, this is a sign of diarrhea (see page 33). You can treat simple digestive disturbances yourself with the help of a diet or simple medications (see If Your Chinchilla Gets Sick, page 33).

Monitoring Nutritional Condition
Because of its thick fur, you cannot judge the nutritional condition of a chinchilla without taking it in your hands. Palpate your chinchilla regularly along the back and over the chest so that you will notice early on if it is too thin. A healthy chinchilla feels slender; it has palpable padding on the ribs and on the spinal column. If you can feel the bones of the spine and the ribs clearly, the animal is too thin. A chinchilla is seldom too fat.

Hair Rings on Males
Hair rings can develop around the penis and must be removed as quickly as possible. Hair and other foreign matter that is caught on the penis will irritate the organ until it can no longer be withdrawn. If the male continually raises his hind end jerkily and cleans his penis conspicuously and eventually vigorously, you must examine it. To do so raise him by the base of the tail (see page 14). You must remove the hair rings and other foreign matter with a fingernail or with a blunt object, perhaps with a pair of *blunted* tweezers. It's easier for two people to do this. If you don't trust yourself with this job, you must have the hair rings removed by a veterinarian.

Cage Cleaning

The cage should be cleaned every 5 to 7 days. Brush out the cage floor, wipe it with clean water, dry it off, and then put in fresh litter.

Check several times a week for damp places in the cage. It can happen that your chinchilla has a urinating station at the point where a climbing branch rises from the cage floor. The litter is wet in this spot, and the dampness will be drawn into the branch. This leads to the development of dangerous molds. Scour the branch with clean hot water and let it dry. Then you can put it back into the cage but in a different place.

One problem in the house is the constant shedding of the cottonlike fine chinchilla hairs. They collect in balls in the cage grating, especially along the back wall. Remove these hair clumps several times weekly with a damp cloth or with a vacuum cleaner. If you use a vacuum cleaner, take your chinchilla into another room so that it won't be frightened by the noise. You should always do this anyway when you vacuum clean. Cleaning the equipment: You need to clean the dried feces only from the sitting boards and the sleeping house.

If your chinchilla has a closed sleeping house, you must renew the wood shavings every few weeks. Chinchillas like their own smell. Examine the litter in the sleeping house for dampness during the weekly cleaning. Damp litter must be removed at once and replaced.

Unfortunately, many sleeping houses are put together with nails. The chinchilla can be injured by nails that have been gnawed free; they must be removed.

The water dispenser must be cleaned at least once weekly with a bottle brush, as must the

Unusual color mutations bred by the author. Left, the light-beige female, Emily, with dark eyes, 9 months old. Right: the silver-spotted male, Idefix, with beautiful white markings on his face, 7 months old.

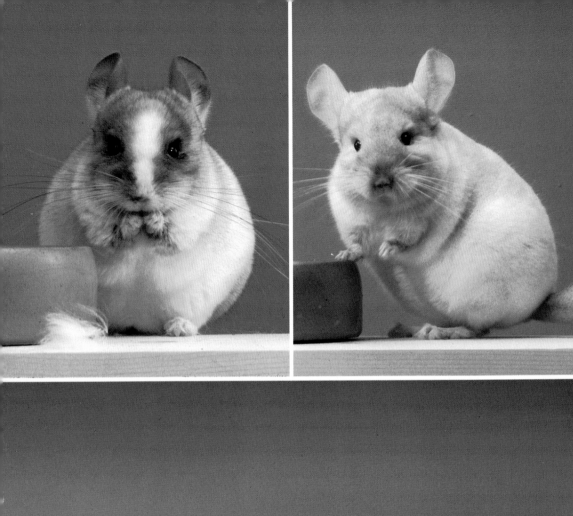

stopper. It's even better if you clean the bottle daily. Provide yourself with a small thin brush for the drinking pipette. Algae—brown, green, or red—grow very easily in the water bottle. The red algae are particularly dangerous and will quickly lead to the death of your animal.

The bath is a constant source of dust. In bathing and in its acrobatics, the chinchilla spreads a fine layer of dust in the vicinity of the cage. You can largely avoid this if you place the bathtub in the cage only for the evening bath. In this short time the dust will also not be substantially contaminated with feces and urine. Renew the dust every few weeks, and clean the bathtub with clean water.

Chinchillas eating. Top left, a silver-spotted male; top right, light-beige female; bottom, light-beige female and silver-spotted male.

Proper Feeding

The chinchilla's gut is adapted to the meager diet of its South American habitat, which includes many indigestible components (see page 32). The chinchilla's gut will remain healthy only if it receives enough roughage—through being fed hay and pellets. Unfortunately, chinchillas quickly get used to preferring treats to the feed that is healthy and wholesome for them. They would much rather eat all fatty and oily foods, like nuts and sunflower seeds, as well as raisins and sweets, cake, and cookies. These foodstuffs have too little roughage. They should only be given in the tiniest amounts; otherwise they are harmful (see Constipation, page 34). An indulgent and undisciplined owner will easily be led into the temptation to feed his or her pet to death.

Basic Feed

Fur breeders went through decades of sometimes bitter experience before they found out what food is best suited to the digestive system of the chinchilla. The breeders established that the basic feed should be special chinchilla pellets, hay, and water.

Pellets: Pellets are a special feed for chinchillas. They are small, greenish brown pressed rods, composed of milled grains, hay, and milk by-products, with vitamins and minerals mixed in. Look for this special feed in the pet store, for there is no equally good substitute for chinchillas. Pay attention to the manufacturing date when you buy. Pellets should not be more than 6 months old when they are used; after 6 months the vitamins will no longer be effective. It's better to buy fresh pellets more often and in smaller quantities. I would like to stress that special chinchilla pellets must be used, not rabbit pellets. Rabbit pellets have too much carbohydrate.

Fur breeders have demonstrated that the prolonged feeding of rabbit pellets produces liver disease in chinchillas. The feeding goal for caged rabbits is fattening, and this goal determines the composition of the rabbit pellets. (Pet rabbits reared exclusively with pellets become fat.) Fattening food is dangerous to the health of the chinchilla.

Hay: The hay should be well seasoned and dry. Dryness is the first commandment for hay! Be careful about storage. It is also important that no mold fungus develops during storage. Funguses produce dangerous diarrhea in chinchillas. It's a good idea to provide air holes in the storage container.

Alfalfa or rabbit hay is quite suitable as feeding material for a chinchilla. You can get it in a pet store. Before you feed the hay, smell it to find out whether it's become damp or moldy. Good hay smells fragrant—to my perception like tobacco—and without a trace of musty or moldy odor. You can easily dry hay that has become damp in the sunshine, or in winter near the radiator, so that you can feed it crackling dry. Don't feed hay that smells musty after drying.

Drinking Water

Drinking water must be provided fresh daily. It should be at room temperature. In most big cities the drinking water contains chlorine; this tap water must be boiled. Mix cider vinegar with the drinking water, a half teaspoon to a cup ($1/4$ liter). The vinegar induces appetite and is healthy for the intestinal flora.

Treats

In taming the chinchilla and in daily play with it it's important to offer the animal some especially beloved food as an inducement. Unfortunately you should only give it the most limited amounts of all the food that are appropriate and that it

Proper Feeding

While eating or gnawing the chinchilla holds large pieces of food or branches in both forepaws.

craves. (Offer only one treat at a time. Avoid overfeeding. The feces must be constantly examined for signs of digestive disturbances! See drawing, page 33.)

Suitable daily treats are: a piece of apple or carrot, a single raisin, or a half a hazelnut or acorn. Feed only the smallest quantities of nuts and raisins. Do not let your little animal's eagerness for these delicacies lead you to feeding it to death. Also suitable are dried and chopped rose hips (available in health-food stores), which you can offer the chinchilla on the palm of your hand. The bark of apple trees and sunflower seeds are also very popular. The pet store carries a mixture just for chinchillas. Occasionally you can also offer the animal a little piece of hard white bread or roll.

Vitamins and Minerals

Many vitamins and minerals are contained in the basic feed. In addition the chinchilla needs calcium. You can sprinkle a calcium preparation over the pellets in the feeding dish; this calcium preparation is available in the pet store. Calcium tablets are also suitable and especially well liked.

You can give the chinchilla some vitamins and minerals in liquid form three times a week. This should be done with the advice of your veterinarian. (Note, however, that pellets specifically identified as chinchilla food are nutritionally balanced, complete foods. Chinchilla pellets do not need supplements — unless your veterinarian prescribes them for your pet.) A mineral stone or salt spool from the pet store will supplement the calcium supply.

Rules for Feeding

Feeding time is at evening. When your chinchilla becomes lively in the evening, provide it with fresh hay, fresh drinking water, and pellets. You can also give it treats at "playtime" during exercise.

The adult chinchilla receives a lightly heaped tablespoon of pellets in its feeding bowl and one or two handfuls of hay in the hayrack in addition. Hay that is lying on the floor of the cage in the litter must be removed every day. It can become dirty or damp and then it is harmful to the chinchilla. At times of much exercise and during pregnancy and lactation, you must increase the allowance of pellets. If you find in the morning that a healthy chinchilla has not eaten all the pellets or has rejected the hay, you must reduce the pellet allowance — not the hay.

For juveniles during the growth period the rules vary because young animals like to eat too many pellets, and then they get diarrhea. Young animals at the age of about 3 months receive a level teaspoon of pellets daily, half in the morning, half at evening. Up to the age of about 6 months, the pellet ration is gradually increased to the adult portion. To accomplish this, the morning portion is lessened and the evening meal gradually increased to the heaping tablespoon of pellets.

Proper Feeding

In the evening the chinchilla gets fresh hay from the hayrack, which is fastened to the inside of the cage screening.

Do not stint the young animals' hay ration; they should receive as much of it as they want morning and evening besides the precisely measured pellets.

Change of feed: Sudden changes in the composition of the feed can lead to constipation or diarrhea in a chinchilla. If possible, you should introduce such changes over several weeks. Mix increasingly larger portions of the new feed into the regular feed. You must also consider this change-over problem if a young chinchilla comes to live with you. If you can, get feed from the pet store or the breeder along with your new animal so you can accustom your chinchilla to its new diet gradually.

Harmful Food

Over and over again in my veterinary practice I have seen chinchillas that have been fed with parrot food and nuts and even with hamster or guinea pig food. I must point out once again that chinchillas gladly eat this food, even prefer it to the suitable feed—but they cannot tolerate it! Sometimes this lack of tolerance appears only after a long time, but then it can be too late and the chinchilla is seriously ill. I must also warn against green feed. Single blades or small leaves of grass, lettuce, or dandelion can be wholesome. In large quantities, however, green food is unhealthy, as experiments at the beginning of the captivity period have demonstrated.

Another hazard is hay harvested in the fall at the second and third mowing. It must be examined meticulously for the leaves of the highly poisonous meadow saffron (autumn crocus). Hay from forest meadows is not suitable, either, because it can contain poisonous ferns.

If Your Chinchilla Gets Sick

Prevention Measures

Chinchillas are basically quite hardy animals. If they are properly fed and maintained, they seldom become ill. To keep your chinchilla healthy, you must observe some ground rules.

• A chinchilla needs absolute quiet during the day. It must be able to sleep in its sleeping house utterly undisturbed. With continual disturbances during the day it becomes nervous and distraught. (See Convulsions, page 35.)
• Sudden changes in the composition of the feed can lead to diarrhea. If possible, introduce changes over several weeks. Mix increasingly larger portions of the new feed into the customary feed. (See Rules for Feeding, page 31.)

Top, normally formed feces; bottom right, indications of constipation; bottom left, indications of dangerously advanced constipation.

• Examine the feces daily. At the first signs of diarrhea (see page 33) or constipation (see page 34), treat the animal immediately. (See drawing.)
• Regularly palpate the back and the chest to check the nourishment status (see page 26).
• Do not feed with old chinchilla pellets. Pay attention to the expiration date (see page 30).
• Use only perfect hay for feeding. Do not feed damp or moldy hay (see page 30).
• Remove daily any hay that is lying on the floor of the cage. Dirty hay leads to diarrhea.

• Change the drinking water daily, and clean the water bottle (see page 30).
• Put fresh gnawing material in the cage regularly (see page 25). The chinchilla can work on it and wear down its constantly growing incisors.

Illnesses of Chinchillas

Diarrhea

Signs of illness: The feces are soft and may be pressed flat, remain stuck to surfaces (for example, the perching boards), and leave behind a greenish or brownish greasy smear.

Possible causes: Damp or moldy hay; algae in the drinking water dispenser; too much greenstuff for food; intolerable green plants; intake of poisonous materials (such as cleaning or washing agents); sudden change of feed; overeating in young animals.

Treatment: Complete withdrawal of food for 24 hours, addition of cider vinegar or Terramycin to drinking water (see page 30); if the feces retain shape, give only hay the next day. On the third day give hay and a quarter of the normal pellet ration. If the feces are still more formed, you can proceed slowly to the normal quantity of pellets. The perches must be cleaned of fecal material daily and thoroughly scoured with clean water; the litter must be renewed daily. If there is no improvement, seek professional help.

If the animal is clearly sick, apathetic, crouches in a corner and doesn't eat, and the diarrhea is severe—that is, liquid and mucous— you must go to the veterinarian immediately. Take a fecal sample with you for a fecal examination.

Prevention: Examine the hay for dampness and development of mold; clean the water dispenser and the drinking pipe regularly. Make sure young animals don't overeat.

If Your Chinchilla Gets Sick

Constipation

Signs of illness: Progressively smaller balls of excrement (see drawing, page 33); dragginess; lack of appetite.

Possible causes: Too many treats; improper feeding with parrot or hamster feed; too little exercise.

Treatment: Cease all treats. Administer the prescribed amount of Karlsbad (mineral salts, from the veterinarian) in drinking water. A tame chinchilla that feels completely at home can be allowed a longer exercise period in the evenings.

If the balls of excrement continue to grow smaller and the chinchilla remains draggy and not interested in eating, you must take it to the veterinarian. Otherwise it can develop an intestinal blockage, which very quickly leads to the death of your animal.

Precautions: Do not overfeed your animal, and do not give it too many treats (see Rules for Feeding, page 31). Let your animal run free every day until it has exhausted its need for movement.

Signs of Health and Illness

	Healthy	Sick
Fur	Uniformly thick, soft, and "fragrant"	Hair broken and falling out, thinning, holes in pelt; scaly and crusty portions of skin; eventually skin becomes visible; greasy all over and gummy or badly matted
Nose	Dry and clean	Wounds; nasal discharge; crusty and scaly
Incisors	Yellow-orange, the lower teeth longer than the upper	Whitish or fragilely translucent; position and length departing from healthy standard (see drawing page 25)
Eyes	Surrounding area dry and clean	Sticky discharge; hair falling out, scaly-crusty skin changes in the region of the eyes
Ears	Clean; smooth ear edges without deposits	Wounds; scales, crust and scurf along the edges of the ear or on the entire ear; yellowish skin
Anal region	Clean	Anal region and underside of the tail smeary or dirty
Feces	Formed (see page 33); perches clean	Soft, smeary or mucous; perches dirty
Nourishment	Chinchilla palpates slim, with detectable padding on the ribs and spinal column	In malnutrition bones of the spine and the ribs feel like those of a skeleton

If Your Chinchilla Gets Sick

Convulsions

Signs of illness: Muscle tremors, muscle cramps, dislocations, or transient failure of locomotion. This convulsive condition is dreadful to see; it can last for some minutes (up to 15).

Possible causes: Calcium or vitamin B deficiency; stress, often in pregnant females.

Treatment: Go to the veterinarian at once. For vitamin B deficiency, injections and addition of vitamin B to the drinking water have been shown to be effective. Increase the calcium intake to a whole tablet daily. The animal must be protected especially carefully from noise during the day.

Prevention: Give your chinchilla a half tablet of calcium daily (see page 31). Be careful that the pellets aren't too old or improperly stored (see page 30). Ensure undisturbed daytime rest for your animal.

Skin Funguses

Signs of illness: Holes in the fur; crustiness, scales, scabs, and scurf on the nose and around the eyes; within a few days these spots spread over the head and to other parts of the body (not to be confused with "fur biting," see page 37).

Possible causes: Skin funguses are very widely distributed in our environment. Unhygienic maintenance of the chinchilla or the addition of an animal from an unfamiliar stock increases the danger of infection.

Treatment: Skin funguses must be treated by a veterinarian immediately. A fungal infection can be healed with additives to the bath dust. A laboratory examination is necessary if the animal is newly acquired—it is important to recognize right away the funguses that are contagious to human beings and to other pets.

Prevention: Clean, hygienic maintenance of the chinchilla. Administer the prescribed amount of fungicide powder (available from the veterinarian) in the bath dust.

Eye Infection

Signs of illness: Milky, watery eye discharge; the area around the afflicted eye is damp and sticky; dried discharge looks like icing; the eye swells shut.

Possible causes: Grains of sand or other foreign bodies, even small wounds, can lead to a connective tissue infection.

Treatment: Go to the veterinarian, who will prescribe an antibiotic salve. This salve should be administered carefully to the eye and the surrounding area three times daily. Carefully clean away the crust from the area around the eye with a paper tissue. The salve must be applied for 3 days more after the eye discharge stops. During the treatment and for at least 1 week afterward, the chinchilla should not have a dust bath. The dust will stick to the region around the eye and produce more irritation.

Prevention: At the slightest sign of eye discharge, discontinue the dust baths for a week.

Colds

Signs of illness: Watery or purulent nasal discharge; breathing difficulty.

Possible causes: Drafts; too high a humidity; stress during transport and during change of environment.

Treatment: The animal must be taken to the veterinarian, who will prescribe appropriate medicine or administer it. Protect the chinchilla especially well to avoid drafts and stress.

Prevention: Don't place the cage in a draft; don't keep the chinchilla in damp rooms; avoid unnecessary transfers from one place to another.

Infectious Diseases

Signs of illness: Lack of appetite; diarrhea in combination with increasing malnutrition; tiredness.

Possible causes: No viral illnesses are specific to chinchillas (as distemper is specific to dogs or feline leukemia to cats). Those illnesses induced by viruses or bacteria that do appear are also infectious to other animals. The agents of infection are everywhere in our environment, and a chinchilla whose resistance is weakened by poor maintenance and feeding patterns is especially vulnerable. A healthy animal, on the other hand, does not fall ill.

Treatment: Go to the veterinarian, who will determine the illness and prescribe the appropriate medication.

Prevention: Proper living conditions, care, and nourishment strengthen the resistance to infectious diseases.

Broken and Abnormally Growing Incisors

Signs of illness: The chinchilla eats more slowly than usual, lets partly chewed pellets fall; saliva flows from the muzzle, the chinchilla "slobbers"; unnatural position of the incisors, incisors too long (see drawing, page 25); not to be confused with anomalies of the molars.

Possible causes: Calcium deficiency during growing period; too little gnawing material; accident—broken teeth have grown back abnormally.

Treatment: Injured incisors must be treated by the veterinarian. Broken off and abnormally growing incisors must be shortened at brief intervals. For all tooth abnormalities the nutritional condition must be constantly monitored—preferably weekly on a kitchen scale. If the chinchilla slowly but steadily loses weight in spite of all efforts, you should consider having it put to sleep so that the animal need not suffer any longer.

Prevention: Sufficient calcium during the growth period (see Vitamins and Minerals, page 31); always provide fresh gnawing materials in the cage; avoid accidents (jumping from too high a height, squeezing in a door, being stepped on) (see Table of Hazards, page 24).

Anomalies of the Molars

Signs of illness: Similar to those of anomalies of the incisors; slow eating, exaggerated chewing, "slobbering," unnatural growth of the incisors (see drawing, page 25).

Causes: Missing number of teeth at birth; uneven wearing of back teeth; jagged edges of back teeth irritate the tongue or the mucous membrane of the cheeks. The incisors can no longer be worn down, they become too long and lead to lockjaw.

Treatment: The jagged edges on the molars must be nipped off or ground off under anesthesia by the veterinarian, as must the incisors. If the jagged edges continue to recur and the animal is in pain, you will be forced to consider putting it to sleep.

Prevention: Faulty configuration of the molars can be hereditary. Animals with such conditions should not be bred.

Wounds

Signs of illness: Open wounds.

Possible causes: Bites, snagging on nails or sharp edges, pinching in doors or windows.

Immediate measures: Dab open wounds with a wound disinfectant and apply wound powder. As a rule the chinchilla will not tolerate a bandage.

Treatment: The wound must be treated by a veterinarian immediately. With open wounds there is the danger of a wound infection, which in chinchillas appears quickly and is tenacious; through gnawing and licking chinchillas worsen the inflammation of small wounds. After several injections of a special antibiotic (for example, chloramphenicol) the chinchilla is soon well again. Minor scratches should be cleaned and disinfected. Apply a dusting powder containing a sulfa drug, or bacitracin ointment may be used.

Prevention: Eliminate dangers that will produce wounds (see Table of Hazards, page 24).

If Your Chinchilla Gets Sick

Broken Bones

Signs of illness: Difficulty in movement, inability to put weight on limbs, unnatural position of limbs; with open breaks the bones themselves are visible.

Possible causes: Accidents of various kinds.

Immediate measures: Put the chinchilla in a small, closed container (cardboard or wooden box), and take it to the veterinarian.

Treatment: Only by the veterinarian! The animal may be left with a slight inhibition of mobility. If the break cannot be healed, the animal must be put to sleep.

Prevention: Eliminate the sources of danger (see Table of Hazards, page 24).

Loss of Weight as a Sign of Severe Illness

Signs: Extreme malnutrition, drooping neck, and steeply hunched back when the animal sits (see drawing below). You can discover increasing malnourishment on a kitchen scale: Even if the animal eats, a weight loss of 0.7 to 1.4 ounces (20 to 40 grams) per week is alarming.

Loss of weight is an extreme sign of chronic illness, such as liver disease or inflammation of the intestines.

Possible causes: Chronic illness, such as liver disease or intestinal inflammation resulting from poor maintenance and, most of all, from wrong feeding.

Treatment: You must let the veterinarian determine the cause of the disease. Perhaps the animal can be healed again with medication and change to appropriate maintenance and feeding. The healing process takes several months.

Prevention: Proper care and feeding is the prerequisite for prevention of this serious illness. Provide for the daytime rest for your animal; avoid stressing it. Give your animal sufficient exercise (see Care and Maintenance, page 21). Never feed it too many treats, and above all don't give it the wrong food (see Harmful Food, page 32). Pay attention to the first signs of an intestinal illness.

Behavioral Disturbances

Fur Biting

The gnawing on the fur of other chinchillas.

Signs: You can't usually observe the actual act of gnawing. The chinchilla has holes in its pelt, and these are usually in places that the animal could not reach on its own body.

Possible causes: In a cage that is too small, in which perhaps mothers and young are kept, the animals get on each other's nerves at times. The young animals can't sufficiently rein in their need for movement. If feed is supplied by a dispenser, the animals can only get it one at a time, so they crowd and scuffle. This fur biting can also appear with grown animals if the cage is too small for all the animals.

Treatment: Give the animals a larger cage, or take individual animals out. If the animals have enough space again, the biting will stop and the fur will grow again.

Prevention: Observe from the very beginning how well the animals tolerate each other in a

If Your Chinchilla Gets Sick

common cage. Provide a larger cage if you are planning to raise chinchillas. Check the fur constantly for holes. At the first signs of fur biting you must react at once.

Chewing on Own Fur

Signs: Holes in the fur; the chewing itself can't usually be observed.

Possible causes: Stress from various factors: unusual noise, especially during the sleeping period in the daytime (constant barking of a new dog in the neighborhood, construction noise, repairs in the house that are accompanied by loud noise). Overcrowded cages: Even if the animals appear to tolerate it, they need enough space; even animals in neighboring cages can develop tensions that result in fur biting. It has also been suggested that inherited disturbances in the hormone balance of the chinchilla may be a cause of fur biting.

Treatment: Provide for the stress-free maintenance of the animal. Consider carefully what changes could have occurred in the environment of the animal in the last weeks: new sounds, new pets, or similar disturbances. Any stress factors that you suspect are disturbances for the chinchilla should be removed.

Prevention: Keep the possibility of all new, loud noises away from the chinchilla. You can place the cage in another, quieter room.

Stereotypical Movements

Signs: Like a tiger in a cage, the chinchilla runs back and forth along the perching board; arriving at the left or right cage wall, it prepares to jump down—but it doesn't and resumes its hurried pacing back and forth.

Possible causes: The cage offers too little space for running and for alternations in jumping.

Treatment and prevention: Put the chinchilla in a larger cage with more perches and climbing branches; give it more exercise every day, and play with it during this time.

Breeding Chinchillas

What You Should Think About Beforehand

The breeding of pets is a source of pride to pet owners. They know then that the animals are comfortable. If you want your chinchillas to have young, however, you must think about some things beforehand:

● You need an especially large cage for keeping a chinchilla pair—or even a small colony (see page 16).
● The sleeping house in the cage must be so large that the mother and her young can fit comfortably in it. The sleeping house should also be closed on all sides—except for the entry hole.
● If you want to have only one brood, you must take the male out of the cage before the birth; otherwise the female will mate again immediately after the birth.
● Placing a buck in the cage just for breeding with one doe is difficult. Weeks or even months may pass before it "works."
● Consider well whether you want to leave the breeding pair together constantly. After several broods (up to three a year) even the strongest female deserves a rest.
● After several broods you will soon have no room for the new young. Make proper arrangements ahead of time for good disposal of the young animals.

The Right Pair

Young animals: If you want to acquire a pair in order to breed them later, it is simplest to bring them together as young animals so they can get acquainted. You must be careful that the female does not become pregnant too young. Maturity, that is, the first heat, comes as early as the age of 4 to 5 months. This is too early for breeding, however, because the animal is not yet fully

Top left, a freshly extruded vaginal plug; top right, an old, dried-up vaginal plug; bottom, various cover plugs that have been expelled by the female.

grown. The female should be 8 to 9 months old before she is allowed to become pregnant. The best thing is to keep the animals in two cages side by side until the female is old enough to breed.

If the female is not in heat (signs of estrus, see page 40), the animals can be left together during exercise.

Adult animals: Bringing two older animals together can be more difficult. Keep them both in separate cages, and place the cages next to each other. If you have the impression that they both will tolerate each other, then place the male in the cage (the largest possible) of the female. In the beginning the female will perhaps act somewhat shy, but as a rule they both get on well together after a time.

A young animal and an older one: A young buck placed with an older female is less overwhelming than is an older buck. It is easier to put such a pair together than it is two grown animals. They become used to each other more quickly. Again, place the animals next to each other in separate cages so that they can get to know each other before you place the buck with the doe.

Breeding Chinchillas

Note: Should a serious antipathy be observed even once between a pair that has been placed together, despite a slow acquaintance period, the animals should be separated again. Chinchillas can be individuals, and they will not let themselves be forced into anything!

Animals That Should Not Be Bred: The Lethal Factor

Certain color combinations (see page 44) are not suitable for breeding. You cannot expect offspring from a pair of black velvets or a pair of brown velvets. The breeding of white with white is also not recommended. These pairs cannot bring healthy offspring into the world. The cause of this is a "lethal factor." Some embryos even die in the mother's body or the female aborts. Other babies are born dead or too weak to survive. One can, however, cross white chinchillas and black and brown velvets successfully with other color lines.

Estrus

The term "estrus" or "heat" is used to describe the female's readiness to mate. This appears for the first time at the age of 4 to 5 months. Chinchilla females come into estrus every 28 to 35 days. Most females are regularly in heat between December and February and in high summer. Accordingly most births take place in May, June, and October. Estrus lasts 3 to 4 days. At the beginning the female usually expels from the vagina an "estrus (or vaginal) plug," which is a waxy plug 1 to 1.2 inches (2.5 to 3 cm) long (see drawing, page 39). You may discover the estrus plug in the cage litter. Estrus is easier to recognize in the opened vagina, which is posi-

tioned crosswise, between the anus and the end of the urinary tract. If the female is not in heat, the vagina is closed (see drawing, page 15).

Mating

Mating usually takes place at night. Sometimes you can also observe it in the evening or in the early morning hours. First the female is reluctant; she rejects the male's advances. The buck chases the doe, and so they both tussle around the cage. Then, during mating, the buck mounts the doe from behind. Copulation takes place many times in one night. The buck ejects a waxy substance into the vagina. This hardens, forming a "cover plug" that temporarily holds the semen inside the doe. In the morning you will find the clumps of hair torn out during the tusseling. If you find the cover plug in the litter, you have certain evidence of a successful mating. The "cover plug" looks very similar to the estrus plug except that it is somewhat smaller (see drawing, page 39).

During mating the buck mounts the doe from behind.

40

Breeding Chinchillas

Pregnancy

The gestation period lasts about 111 days. This is unusually long for a rodent—golden hamsters deliver their young in 16 to 18 days. The chinchilla pair lives very harmoniously together during this period. They sleep nestled closely together. During pregnancy the female needs an especially large amount of rest. Discontinue·the weight-monitoring palpation during this period. Give her fresh pellets to be sure that she receives enough vitamins, and provide sufficient calcium in the diet.

In the last weeks of pregnancy the mother often sleeps lying on her side. This is an unfamiliar, even frightening sight, because the animal looks as though she'd died. This is normal behavior, however, and a certain sign of pregnancy.

Birth

Birth occurs at night or in the early morning. If you come to the cage in the morning and discover that the mother animal's muzzle is bloody and her forepaws smeared with blood, it is a sure sign that the birth is finished.

As a rule there are no difficulties during the birth. Preliminary pain announces the beginning; the female moans, writhes, and stretches and emits sounds of pain. Normally the stressful, painful phase doesn't last long, about half an hour. Finally the female carefully draws out the young with her teeth. When there are multiple births (three to four young) the birthing can take several hours. When it is over, the female eats the fleshy afterbirth. In doing so her muzzle and forepaws become smeared with blood.

The birth takes place in a corner of the cage or in the sleeping house. In multiple births the mother moves about the cage, so the births can

A few days after birth the little chinchillas explore the cage curiously, but they keep coming back to the protection of their mother.

occur in different places. The firstborn animals follow the mother and slip under her belly seeking warmth.

Complications of Birth

Disturbances of birth seldom appear, assuming, of course, that the female is not disturbed during that time by human beings or other pets. Sometimes, however, your help as "obstetrician" is necessary.

● There can be difficulties if an infant is too large and remains stuck in the vagina or if a baby has already died within the mother's body. Then the birth will not proceed. If you notice this, you must consult with a veterinarian immediately.

● In multiple births it may happen that the single babies come too quickly, one after the other. Then a baby cannot be kept warm enough and be licked dry, because the mother is already busy with the next one. The damp infant can die of hypothermia as a result. Carefully take out the baby and warm it in your hands. Breathe on it until it is dry. As soon as it can stand by itself, give it back to the mother.

● Sometimes the eyes of a newborn are stuck closed so that it cannot open them (chinchillas come into the world with full vision!). Apply some eye salve to the crack between the eyelids and then draw the eyelids carefully apart.

Development of the Young Animals

The first hours: The damp newborns slip under the mother's belly and dry in a short time in the warmth and the mother's licking. Already the young are emitting a soft *peeping,* a kind of contact sound. By means of gentle biting in the neck area the mother awakens the "life spirit" of the newborn. The youngsters react to this with a somewhat louder squeaking. It always seems to me as if the mother tests uses this neck bite to test whether her youngster is healthy and capable of living.

Chinchillas are precocial. They come into the world fully developed, independent, with fur and sight. Their weight at birth is between 1 and 2 ounces (30 and 55 grams), around 1.4 ounces (40 grams) on the average. The newborn chinchilla is scarcely larger than a matchbox. Even after a few hours it runs everywhere after its mother. If both parents are in the cage after the birth, the baby will also seek warmth and protection from the father, who takes it in lovingly.

I have already pointed out (see page 39) that shortly after the birth the female will mate again immediately. If you want to prevent this, you must take the male out of the common cage.

The first few days: When the little one is a few days old, it will climb up the cage wall; it hops onto low impediments, onto the sleeping house and the lower perching boards. If the parents are tame and trusting, take the infant that is a few days old into your hands every now and then so that it will quickly become comfortable with

you. Be careful; the youngster is as slippery as quicksilver and may spring quickly out of your hand. Close both hands carefully around the animal and hold it in this hollow. Speak gently to it while you are holding it.

Feeding the Newborn

In its very first days of life the newborn nibbles on blades of hay and soon also on pellets. Besides the mother's milk it also very slowly and routinely takes in solid food: The changeover from mother's milk to solid food goes smoothly. Thus the stomach and the intestines of the small chinchilla gradually get used to the difficult-to-digest ingredients of the diet. After 3 weeks the infant has doubled its birth weight. You need not pay much attention to the feeding of the babies in the first 6 weeks. The young will eat the mother's food, just as much as they need. Therefore give the mother a little more hay and pellets than usual each day.

Separation from the Mother

After 6 weeks the chinchilla young no longer need the mother's milk. Leave them with the mother for 2 to 3 weeks longer. You can keep the young in a common cage even longer if the cage is large enough. It is quite charming to observe the peaceful social life of a family.

When you separate the young from the mother at the age of 6 to 8 weeks, you must keep a close watch on the quantities of food for the young animals and measure it carefully. The young overeat on the pellets very easily and then get diarrhea (see page 33). For this reason, until the young are 5 or 6 months old, I feed them in the morning and evening in the following quantities: First a handful of hay for each; when they have taken the edge off the first hunger with it, 1/2 teaspoon of pellets for each, increasing with age up to 1 whole teaspoon of pellets.

Breeding Chinchillas

Note: If you sell a young animal, make the buyer aware of this "overeating aspect" and also bear it in mind yourself if you buy a young animal, which is usually offered at the age of 2½ to 5 months (see Rules for Feeding, page 31).

In the first few days the baby is fed with the aid of a bottle (top) or an eyedropper (bottom).

Feeding Large Litters

In the case of births of three or four young, often the mother's milk is not enough for all the babies. Then you must help the mother because otherwise the young will bite her teats in the battle for the milk source. Mix bottled milk (7.5% fat content) with hot drinking water in the proportion of 1:1. Put this body-temperature milk supplement in a feeding bottle (available at a pet dealer's). Take the newborn in one hand and feed it with the other (see accompanying drawing). For larger animals simply hold out the bottle and the animal will nurse on it all by itself. You can also try to feed with a pipette or an eyedropper: Be careful. The babies swallow the wrong way very easily and then get milk in the lungs, which is fatal!

Raising Motherless Young

If the mother dies, you must quickly find a substitute mother, a "wet-nurse." A suitable mother is one with only one baby of the same age as your offspring. If you can't find a substitute mother, you can try to feed the newborns yourself. Sometimes this is successful. Provide yourself with milk formula for dogs or cats from the pet store. In the first days the young must be fed every 2 hours with freshly mixed warmed formula. Afterward massage the belly gently with a finger so that the intestines will be stimulated. After a few days the newborns receive additional solid food in small quantities: hay and pellets. The formula should be given only every 3 hours during the second week of life. The animals need formula up to the age of 5 to 6 weeks, with a little bit less each day in the course of these weeks.

The chinchilla needs fresh material to gnaw on regularly, branches, for example, so that its teeth will not become too long.

The warmth of the mother is missing for the newborn. Put it in a wooden box with hay, and place the box in the vicinity of a radiator. Temperatures of 68 to 72°F (20 to 22°C) are necessary so that the baby doesn't die of hypothermia.

Mutations — Color Variations

Besides the color of wild chinchillas, there are a multitude of color variations. The fur breeders call the color of the animals in the wild "standard." The standard skin color ranges from a bright gray to a dark, almost anthracite-colored gray. The underside of the body is light; it can be very contrasting and go almost into white.

Since the 1950s there have been more and more new colors introduced by the fur breeders worldwide:

● White was one of the first sensations: Albinos (white animals with red eyes), white with dark-tipped hairs, resembling the chinchilla-Persian cats.
● Silver: Somewhat darker than chinchilla-Persian cats, white fur background with darkish tipped hairs, like the Persian cat silver shaded. The silvers may have spots.
● Black: Black velvet — black with a light underside.
● Beige: In various shadings, such as cream and sand.
● Brown: Uniformly brown.
● Brown velvet: Dark purple-brown upper side and light underside, similar to black velvet.

The way all these colors are developed, that is, the genetic crosses that produce them, is a special science that is of little significance to the keeper of a single animal or the hobby breeder who breeds only on a small scale. Anyone who wishes to learn more about the color variations can pursue it in the specialists' literature (see Bibliography, page 54).

To avoid disappointment, however, you should know that you can expect no offspring from certain color combinations, such as with a pair of black velvets or brown velvets (see The Lethal Factor, page 40). You can cross these velvets successfully with other colors, however.

The daily bath. The chinchilla first sniffs its bathtub, which is filled with Special Chinchilla Sand (above). You can tell how much this gray chinchilla is enjoying its "bath" (below).

Understanding Chinchillas

Chinchillas and Their Relatives

Chinchillas belong to the rodents, the most varied order of all the mammals. Close relatives are the familiar guinea pigs, but also the lesser known agouti and the capybara.

The chinchilla that is offered as a fur-bearing animal, and now also as a pet in the pet stores, belongs to the species of small chinchillas and is a cross between the short-tailed chinchilla *(Chinchilla chinchilla boliviana,* also called *Chinchilla brevicaudata)* and the long-tailed chinchilla *(Chinchilla lanigera).* In appearance, therefore, it outweighs the compact short-tailed chinchilla, which is very seldom imported as a breeding animal, and the long-tailed chinchilla, with its elongated body and quite large ears. For readers interested in zoology there follows a short overview of the classification of the chinchilla.

The genus Chinchilla in the narrower sense *(Chinchilla)* is divided into two species and three subspecies.

First species: Short-tailed chinchilla *(Chinchilla chinchilla).*

Subspecies: King chinchilla *(Chinchilla chinchilla chinchilla).* In fur-breeding circles this legendary subspecies is also called the true chinchilla or the real chinchilla. It has a body length of almost 16 inches (40 cm), and its fur is of an extraordinary quality. These animals have probably been completely extinct for centuries. The single stuffed example can be seen in the Senckenberg Museum in Frankfurt-am-Main, West Germany.

A standard-color chinchilla. Warning: wool is not at all recommended as a plaything!

A short-tailed chinchilla *(Chinchilla chinchilla boliviana).* This species with compact body, large head, and small ears is very seldom imported and crossed.

The small, short-tailed chinchilla *(Chinchilla chinchilla boliviana)* is very seldom kept in human captivity today; the free-living animals are largely extinct.

Second species: Long-tailed chinchilla or small chinchilla *(Chinchilla lanigera).* This species is frequently kept in human care; the free-living animals are largely extinct.

Zoologists divide the long-tailed chinchilla into three types. These derive from various territories of origin or growth forms. Accordingly we differentiate between the La Plata type, the Costina type, and the Raton type (dwarf chinchilla).

The Chinchilla's Habitat

Chinchillas are native to South America. They live in the rocky caves of the Andes to elevations of 1640 feet (5000 meters) in the countries of Peru, Bolivia, Chile, and Argentina. Their habitat is in natural rock crevices and caves in inhospitable—for humans, almost inaccessible— thorny, barren areas with scant humidity and wide temperature swings between day and night, far away from water sources and often dry for months at a time. To fill their need for moisture the animals graze on the morning dew on the grasses and on water-retaining cactuses and their fruits. Their thick, soft fur not only protects them from extremes of heat and cold but is also a good protection against evaporation.

Chinchillas are active at dusk and during the night—that is, at these times they are almost constantly in motion and busy with hunting for food. When the morning sun appears, they seek their underground homes and remain hidden until the sun sinks below the tops of the mountains. To my knowledge there are no actual reports of the chinchillas' way of life in the literature. It is worthwhile repeating what Alfred Edmund Brehm wrote so graphically about the chinchilla, at that time almost unknown, in his *Illustrated Animal Lives* in 1864:

"The traveler who climbs the cordillera of the western coast of South America vouchsafes, if he has reached a height of eight to twelve thousand feet, that often all the rocks for miles around. . . . are covered with these chinchillas. In Peru, Bolivia, and Chile these animals must be numerous everywhere; for we have learned from travelers that during one day they have passed thousands. . . . They stir around on the apparently entirely bare rock walls, moving with uncommon speed and agility. With surprising ease they climb the walls here and there, though these seem to offer no foothold. They climb 20 to 30 feet straight up with such dexterity and speed that one can scarcely follow them with one's eyes. . . . A rock wall which is covered with hundreds looks dead and empty the moment one fires a shot at them. . . . Sometimes it happens that a traveler who, without doing anything to harm them, stops to rest at that elevation, is immediately surrounded by our rock-dwellers. The entire stone becomes more and more lively; out of every crack, out of every crevice peeps a head. The most curious and trusting chinchillas dare to come closer and finally dart fearlessly under the legs of the waiting mules. . . . All observers agree with the assertion that these animals understand masterfully how to live in the most desolate and dismal mountain regions, and as well how to offer diversion and amusement to the lonely and forsaken humans who have withdrawn there."

The Family and the Group

Travelers in the last century collected large groups of chinchillas. It is thus demonstrated that in their natural surroundings chinchillas live in large colonies. These colonies might consist of many family groups. In Grzimek's *Encyclopedia of the Animal Kingdom* (see Bibliography, page 54), it is reported that chinchillas are monogamous. This seems to me believable only so long as there are no mature female offspring there. In my experience, the mother will not drive the daughters off. There appears to be no conflict if there is enough room available for them all to live together. I consider it probable that the father will drive off the male offspring as they mature.

The Home

Chinchillas use the natural faults in rocks as hiding places; they do not dig their own holes. It has been observed that they share their burrows with other rodents, for example the chinchilla rat. The adjacent passageways and holes of these other cohabitants will then also be lived in. The inside of the hole is very dry and clean. The entrance usually lies deeper than the hole, so that no dampness can trickle in. In the vicinity of the entrance there will be a kind of a toilet, the common defecation place for the inhabitants of the hole.

Understanding Chinchillas

Natural Diet

For nourishment the chinchilla feeds on meager prairie grasses, fruit, the leaves and bark of small shrubs and bushes with much tannic acid, such as roots, stems, leaves, and fruits, and the fleshly, water-rich insides of some species of cactus. Especially beloved are the good-tasting guillaves, the fruit of the quisco, a widely distributed cactus in the territories inhabited by chinchillas. Its stems, which point toward the heavens like fingers, are covered with numerous thorns and can reach a height of 13 to 16 feet (4 to 5 meters). Inside, this cactus has a woody tube, which gives it its upright form. Its fruits fall to the ground when they are ripe. Often, however, the chinchillas can't wait for this development to get to their beloved delicacy. They gnaw the roots of the quisco, get into its woody conduction system, climb high inside, and at different heights gnaw windows through the stem and its outer covering and so get to the desired fruit. In the vicinity of chinchilla colonies there are cactuses that are completely perforated in this manner.

Chinchillas meet their need for fluid by means of food and the morning dew on the grasses.

Natural Enemies

Natural enemies are the eagle and hawk at dusk and most of all the owl, who flies soundlessly at night. The chinchillas are also the natural prey of the fox and are occasionally hunted by the marten. As one can see, the natural enemies of the chinchilla in its own habitat are not very numerous.

The Human Threat

The most dangerous enemy of the chinchilla is the human being. The minimal hunting by the native Amerindians did not endanger the existence of the chinchilla. This situation changed after colonization by the Spanish and the subsequent increased demand for chinchilla pelts. Hunters and mountain dwellers drove the initially guilelessly curious little animals to ever more unreachable high regions of the Andes. Hunting with horsehair slings and stones almost led to the extinction of the chinchilla. At the beginning of this century the demand for chinchilla skins was so great that in 1905, for example, from the Chilean port of Coquimbo alone, 216,000 skins were shipped. Therefore, in 1918, South American governments placed an export embargo on chinchilla pelts, but it was too late to keep the chinchillas from dying out in most of their natural habitat. How many chinchillas live in South America today no one knows. They are included in Appendix I of the Washington Endangered Species Agreement, an international agreement for the protection of animal and plant species that are endangered or are threatened with extinction. This means that any trade in wild chinchillas is forbidden. For the pet keeper these protection measures have no meaning, for all the chinchillas offered by pet stores or breeders come from breeding, and these may be traded without problems. In the last years animal protectors and zoologists have even attempted to re-establish chinchillas in their South American Andean habitat. Naturally-colored (standard) animals, the offspring of animals bred for fur, are placed in especially suitable areas that have been set aside in a (it is to be hoped) successful attempt to make amends for the mistakes of the past.

Understanding Chinchillas

The Body Language of Chinchillas

<u>Hopping and jumping:</u> A tame chinchilla charms with its artlessness and curiosity. A new living space or a new piece of furniture will immediately be hoppingly explored and sniffed. Chinchillas are very lively animals; nevertheless, because of their hopping way of movement, they appear to be somewhat diffident. Like kangaroos, they spring with their powerfully developed back legs. Only during slow forward movement are the short, underdeveloped front legs also used. In jumping the tail serves as a rudder; stretched out behind it holds the chinchilla in balance in the air.

<u>Eating:</u> The front paws are very deft "hands." With them the chinchilla picks up food and moves it to its mouth. Pellets and blades of hay are mostly taken in one paw and eaten—it looks incredibly human! Large pieces are held in both paws to eat. Chinchillas eating are a charming sight: They sit on the hind legs, with the upper body upright, holding the food in the front paws, biting off and chewing, obviously comfortable.

A strange animal is first sniffed thoroughly.

<u>The test bite:</u> Every object new to the chinchilla is tested for edibility. After the first test bite the item is dropped or is eaten. Therefore you must always keep an eye on the animal during exercise. If you stick a finger through the cage wire, a more or less gentle test bite promptly follows—after all, it could be something edible. This tentative bite has nothing to do with real biting, but all the same it can be uncomfortable for the human.

<u>Contact survey:</u> A strange chinchilla will at first be sniffed (see drawing, page 50). If the animals tolerate each other, they will soon crouch together on a perching board. An unwelcome newcomer will be attacked and chased through the cage—or driven off with urine spray.

For protection against an unwished-for human or another chinchilla, the animal stands up straight and sprays urine.

<u>Fear:</u> When the chinchilla is afraid, it will cower, huddled in the corner of the cage. If it gets into an altercation with another chinchilla or an enemy, it is to the chinchilla's advantage that its hair is very loosely attached. In nature this feature often saves the animal from the lethal grip of a predator. If you do not quite catch it when

you are trying to capture it, you will hold only a tuft of hair in your hand. This may have something to do with the phenomenon of "fear shedding."

Defense: Chinchillas react to other chinchillas or to humans with urine spraying if they wish to defend themselves (see drawing). If you want to take a not-very-trusting animal out of the cage, it may, cornered, stand up straight on its hind legs and spray urine against the threatening hand. If you are bending into the cage during such a capture, you get a load of urine square in the face.

The Language of Sounds

The contact sound: Newborn chinchillas are "talkier" than grown-up animals. If a birth has taken place during the night, upon entering my chinchilla room in the morning I immediately hear the fine, soft peeping of the chinchilla babies. For inexperienced chinchilla keepers this soft contact sound is scarcely noticeable. Clearer is the noise that answers the "animating bite" of the mother (see page 42); out of this clear squeaking develops what I call the don't-hurt-me sound of the young animal.

The don't-hurt-me sound: The young continue to use this sound all during the months that they are growing up. It will always be used if the youngster is crowded by the grown-ups, stepped on, or pressed against the cage wall. It bursts out of it when it is captured, in the crowding at the feed dish, and sometimes also if the young one is squeezing through a narrow crack, for example between the cage and the sleeping box. This high squeaking informs the adult animals on approach that the opposite number is a harmless young animal. Sometimes I have been able to determine that the animals that use this sound frequently and apparently without ground—for instance at the tiniest little crowding in the cage—later become especially fearful and nervous chinchillas.

The defense sound: Expressions of bad humor to a partner, a cage neighbor, or even to the outstretched human hand can be expressed in a defensive sound, which is short and almost barking. This sound seems to mean something like "Leave me alone," or "Beat it."

The warning cry: The chinchilla sometimes reacts to unusual sounds with a loud, shrill warning cry, a kind of a whistle. This cry wakens the whole brood and can produce a definite riot. If you speak to them as a trusted human with a soft, quiet voice, the excitement quickly dies down, however.

The coaxing sound: A chinchilla pair often come to an understanding with a coaxing contact sound. These soft, high grunts from both animals confirm their suitability for each other.

The Chinchilla's Sensory Perceptions

I have not been able to find exact scientific statements about what follows. From my own observation and my empathy for the biology of these animals I would like to draw the following conclusions:

Hearing: The hearing ability of the chinchilla seems to me to be very well developed. Thus you may not let yourself be misled into thinking that properly kept chinchillas in their daily sleep phase "tune out" and do not react to ordinary, or louder, sounds. They are disturbed in sleep by unaccustomed sounds, or even softer sounds. They waken or react with the warning cry.

Seeing: Like almost all crepuscular and nocturnal animals, chinchillas have particularly large eyes. With them they can also see something in the twilight and in the dark. I have the impression, however, that they cannot rely particularly well on their sense of sight. They can move very well on jumps of 16 to 20 inches (40 to 50 cm), but they also dare to jump from heights that can injure them. Chinchillas, in my experience, are careful animals; one cannot describe them as daring except when they are driven into a panic. From this I deduce that in jumps from too great a height they are no longer able to judge the distance. Therefore the pet owner must be careful and prevent jumps from the arm to the floor, for example.

Feeling: The chinchilla has whiskers at the end of its muzzle, a "moustache" like a cat's. With their help the chinchilla can find its way about even in the dark.

Smelling and tasting: I can say very little about the acuity of the sense of smell. Chinchillas can differentiate their own children from those of a stranger by the scent. When new food is offered it is always sniffed first. In addition, however, taste also decides whether it is edible. One test bite and the food will be dropped if it doesn't appear to be tasty. If the food tastes good, it will be eaten to the end. I have already mentioned many times that chinchillas love to eat "junk food." The chinchilla's taste sense is of course different from the human's. Professor Kraft writes that even bitter-tasting pills are often taken voluntarily. One should bear this in mind when administering a necessary medication (see If Your Chinchilla Gets Sick, page 33) and try first to see if the chinchilla will take the medicine by itself.

Appendix

Bibliography and Useful Addresses

Bowen, Edwin G., and Ross W. Jenkins, Chinchillas, History, Husbandry, Marketing: Hackensack, New Jersey, 1969.

Kennedy, A.H., Chinchilla Diseases and Ailments: Ontario, 1970.

For information regarding sources of pets, supplies, etc.

Gail Sendom
Empress Chinchilla Breeders Corp.
P.O. Box 402
Morrison, CO 80465

Kathy Mihalcik
Princeton Process, Inc.
501 South Main Street
Spring City, PA 19475

Chinchilla with young.

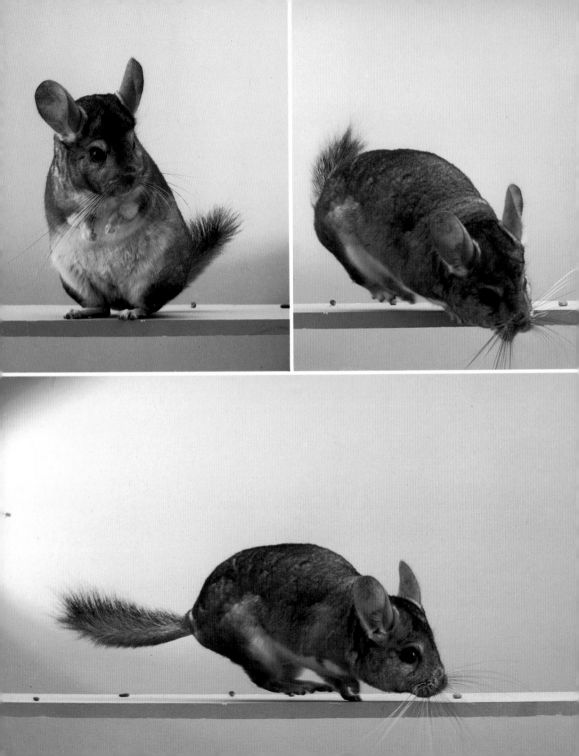

Credits/Note and Warning

The color photographs on the cover show
Front: Chinchilla on its hind legs
Inside front: Tame chinchilla
Inside back: Chinchilla on its hind legs.
Back: Top: Tame standard-color (silver gray) chinchilla; bottom left: white chinchilla; bottom right: brown chinchilla.
The photographer: Karin Skogstad

The author
Maike Röder-Thiede is a practicing veterinarian. She has kept and bred chinchillas as house pets for many years.

Note and Warning

This book deals with the keeping and care of chinchillas as pets. In working with these animals injuries can occur through scratches or bites. Have such wounds treated by a doctor at once.

As a result of unhygienic living conditions, chinchillas can develop skin funguses that are contagious to humans and other animals (see page 35). Have the infected animal treated by a veterinarian at once, and go to the doctor yourself at the slightest suspicion. When buying an animal, watch particularly carefully for the signs of a skin fungal infection (see page 35).

Chinchillas are rodents and must be watched very carefully during the necessary and regular exercise period in the house. To avoid life-threatening electrical accidents, be particularly careful that your chinchilla does not gnaw on any electrical wires.

Phases of a chinchilla's jump. First it becomes alert (top left), then it looks in the direction of the jump (top right), and finally it jumps (bottom).

Index

Index

Index

Perfect for Pet Owners!

PET OWNER'S MANUALS

Over 50 illustrations per book
(20 or more color photos),
72-80 pp., paperback.
AFRICAN GRAY PARROTS (3773-1)
AMAZON PARROTS (4035-X)
BANTAMS (3687-5)
BEAGLES (3829-0)
BEEKEEPING (4089-9)
BOXERS (4036-8)
CANARIES (2614-4)
CATS (2421-4)
CHINCHILLAS (4037-6)
CHOW-CHOWS (3952-1)
COCKATIELS (2889-9)
COCKATOOS (4159-3)
DACHSHUNDS (2888-0)
DOBERMAN PINSCHERS (2999-2)
DWARF RABBITS (3669-7)
FEEDING AND SHELTERING
    BACKYARD BIRDS (4252-2)
FEEDING AND SHELTERING
    EUROPEAN BIRDS (2858-9)
FERRETS (2976-3)
GERBILS (3725-1)
GERMAN SHEPHERDS (2982-8)
GOLDEN RETRIEVERS (3793-6)
GOLDFISH (2975-5)
GUINEA PIGS (2629-2)
HAMSTERS (2422-2)
LABRADOR RETRIEVERS (3792-8)
LHASA APSOS (3950-5)
LIZARDS IN THE TERRARIUM
    (3925-4)
LONG-HAIRED CATS (2803-1)
LOVEBIRDS (3726-X)
MICE (2921-6)
MUTTS (4126-7)
MYNAS (3688-3)
PARAKEETS (2423-0)
PARROTS (2630-6)
PERSIAN CATS (4405-3)
PIGEONS (4044-9)
PONIES (2856-2)
POODLES (2812-0)
RABBITS (2615-2)

SCHNAUZERS (3949-1)
SHEEP (4091-0)
SHETLAND SHEEPDOGS (4264-6)
SIBERIAN HUSKIES (4265-4)
SNAKES (2813-9)
SPANIELS (2424-9)
TROPICAL FISH (2686-1)
TURTLES (2631-4)
YORKSHIRE TERRIERS (4406-1)
ZEBRA FINCHES (3497-X)

NEW PET HANDBOOKS

Detailed, illustrated profiles (40-60
color photos), 144 pp., paperback.
NEW AQUARIUM HANDBOOK
    (3682-4)
NEW BIRD HANDBOOK (4157-7)
NEW CAT HANDBOOK (2922-4)
NEW COCKATIEL HANDBOOK
    (4201-8)
NEW DOG HANDBOOK (2857-0)
NEW DUCK HANDBOOK (4088-0)
NEW FINCH HANDBOOK (2859-7)
NEW GOAT HANDBOOK (4090-2)
NEW PARAKEET HANDBOOK
    (2985-2)
NEW PARROT HANDBOOK (3729-4)
NEW RABBIT HANDBOOK (4202-6)
NEW SOFTBILL HANDBOOK
    (4075-9)
NEW TERRIER HANDBOOK
    (3951-3)

CAT FANCIER'S SERIES

Authoritative, colorful guides (over
35 color photos), 72 pp., paperback.
BURMESE CATS (2925-9)
LONGHAIR CATS (2923-2)

FIRST AID FOR PETS

Fully illustrated, colorful guide, 20 pp.,
Hardboard with hanging chain and
    index tabs.
FIRST AID FOR YOUR CAT (5827-5)
FIRST AID FOR YOUR DOG (5828-3)

REFERENCE BOOKS

Comprehensive, lavishly illustrated
references (60-300 color photos),
136-176 pp., hardcover & paperback.
AQUARIUM FISH SURVIVAL
    MANUAL (5686-8), hardcover
AUSTRALIAN FINCHES, THE
    COMPLETE BOOK OF (6091-1),
    hardcover
BEST PET NAME BOOK EVER, THE
    (4258-1), paperback
CAT CARE MANUAL (5765-1),
    hardcover
COMMUNICATING WITH YOUR
    DOG (4203-4), paperback
COMPLETE BOOK OF
    BUDGERIGARS (6059-8),
    hardcover
COMPLETE BOOK OF PARROTS
    (5971-9), hardcover
DOG CARE, THE COMPLETE BOOK
    OF (4158-5), paperback
DOG CARE MANUAL (5764-3),
    hardcover
GOLDFISH AND ORNAMENTAL
    CARP (5634-5), hardcover
HORSE CARE MANUAL (5795-3),
    hardcover
LABYRINTH FISH (5635-3),
    hardcover
NONVENOMOUS SNAKES (5632-9),
    hardcover
WATER PLANTS IN THE AQUARIUM
    (3926-2), paperback

GENERAL GUIDE BOOKS

Heavily illustrated with color photos,
144 pp., paperback.
COMMUNICATING WITH YOUR DOG
    (4203-4)
DOGS (4158-5)

ISBN prefix: 0-8120

Order from your favorite book or pet store

Barron's Educational Series, Inc. • P.O. Box 8040, 250 Wireless Blvd., Hauppauge, NY 11788
Call toll-free: 1-800-645-3476, in NY: 1-800-257-5729 • In Canada: Georgetown Book Warehouse
34 Armstrong Ave., Georgetown, Ont. L7G 4R9 • Call toll-free: 1-800-668-4336

"A solid bet for first-time pet owners"
—Booklist

We've taken all the best features of our popular Pet Owner's Manuals and added *more* expert advice, *more* sparkling color photographs, *more* fascinating behavioral insights, and fact-filled profiles on the leading breeds. Indispensable references for pet owners, ideal for people who want to compare breeds before choosing a pet. Over 120 illustrations per book—55 to 60 in full color!

"Stunning"
—Roger Caras
Pets & Wildlife

Ulrike Müller **The New Cat Handbook**

Includes a Special Section on Cat "Language" and Behavior

Choosing a Cat • Care & Feeding • Health • Breeding • Showing

BARRON'S

• Data on All Major Breeds • 130 Color Photos and Drawings

Hans-J. Ullmann **The New Dog Handbook**

Choosing a Dog • Training • Care & Feeding • Health • Understanding Dogs

With profiles of 60 breeds, plus 130 color photos and drawings

Christa Koepff **The New Finch Handbook**

Purchase • Care & Feeding • Health • Breeding • Understanding Finches

BARRON'S

Barron's Educational Series, Inc.
P.O. Box 8040, 250 Wireless Blvd., Hauppauge, NY 11788
Call toll-free: 1-800-645-3476, in NY: 1-800-257-5729
In Canada: Georgetown Book Warehouse
34 Armstrong Ave., Georgetown, Ont. L7G 4R9
Call toll-free: 1-800-668-4336

Barron's ISBN prefix: 0-8120

BARRON'S